CRE
CONNE
for CATECHISTS
from TO
A Z

JANET SCHAEFFLER

Catholic
social
teaching

TWENTY
THIRD *23rd*
PUBLICATIONS
www.23rdpublications.com

TWENTY-THIRD PUBLICATIONS
A Division of Bayard
One Montauk Avenue, Suite 200
New London, CT 06320
(860) 437-3012 or (800) 321-0411
www.23rdpublications.com

ISBN 978-1-58595-748-4

Cover image: ©iStockphoto.com/simonvox

Library of Congress Catalog Card Number: 2009926108
Printed in the U.S.A.

CONTENTS

Introduction 1

Advocacy 4

Biblical-based 6

Convoy learning 8

Discuss and debate 10

Examination of conscience 12

Family-friendly service
    opportunities 14

Games of simulation 18

Hunger crisis 21

Imagine 25

Journal 27

Keep connected 29

Link your celebration of sacraments
    and Catholic social teaching 31

Memorial celebrations 34

Notice the news and television 37

Observe Earth Day 39

Place peace at the top of your list
    of priorities 42

Quiet time for reflection 48

Research 50

Skills building. 53

Tell the stories 56

Utilize helpful resources. 59

Voice your opinions. 62

Widen your world 65

Xplore why we engage in service
    and advocacy 69

Your witness. 71

Zoom in on parish/community
    opportunities 73

From Jesus...to us 75

INTRODUCTION

A four-year-old said to his dad, "Daddy, when we go to church, you are no longer my daddy; you are my brother."

When her brother was struck and injured by a car, a little girl was asked to give blood. After the transfusion, she asked the doctor, "When do I die?"

"You're not going to die," the surprised doctor replied.

"I thought if you gave your blood away, you die," the brave little voice explained. So why did she let them take her blood? "Well, he's my brother," she said.

These two small children, although they probably can't articulate it, have a beginning—and very deep—understanding of the principles behind the Gospel values and social teachings of the Catholic Church.

As they grow, their families, the Church, and their faith formation programs will continue to help develop and nurture that life of service, call to justice, and the understanding of the human community (and all of creation) as united and interdependent.

In our parishes and catechetical programs, we are doing a wonderful job of calling children, youth, and adults to service and outreach opportunities. At times, though, something might be lacking. We always need to make connections. We need to connect our actions to the foundations. We need to connect our actions to the reasons we are doing them.

All of social action and outreach is rooted in Scripture and in the ministry of Jesus. Those stories and passages need to be alive for all of us.

Through the years, especially the last 120 years, the Church has developed a rich and comprehensive treasure of wisdom about building a just society and living lives of holiness amid the challenges of modern society. The *Catechism of the Catholic Church* reminds us:

> The Church's social teaching comprises a body of doctrine, which is articulated as the Church interprets events in the course of history, with the assistance of the Holy Spirit, in the light of the whole of what has been revealed by Jesus Christ. (#2422)

The principles and actions to which we are called in Catholic social teaching are not "just nice things to do" when we have time; they are not at the periphery of our lives. They are who we are called to be.

It is the very essence of who we are, because:

- We are responding to the mandate to serve, to justice as Jesus lived.

- We develop a relationship with people whose life experience is different from ours (yet, we are all the same), thus living the reality of the communion of saints.

- We are living our baptism, which anointed us priest, prophet, and king—people living a life of discipleship, a life working for the coming of the reign of God.

Several years ago the U.S. bishops highlighted some of the key themes that are at the heart of our Catholic social tradition:

- the life and dignity of the human person
- the call to family, community, and participation
- the rights and responsibilities of the human person
- the option for the poor and vulnerable
- the dignity of work and the rights of workers
- solidarity
- care for God's creation

Listed here are some ideas, processes, and projects—from A to Z—which can be easily incorporated into:

- catechetical/faith formation sessions and
- ideas for catechists to send home for use in the family

and, hopefully, all these will trigger even more creative ideas (for children, youth, spouses, and families).

A

ADVOCACY

Catholic social teaching calls us to two actions: direct service (e.g., contributing to the Giving Tree, working at a soup
kitchen) and advocacy. Advocacy is working to remove the
cause, going to the deeper problem. This is often done
through letter-writing, emails, and phone calls to state and
national legislators, problem-solving groups, and action
groups; it requires much dedication and risk-taking. Which
issues of concern can you be an advocate for?

This is often also referred to as the two feet of outreach:
charity and justice. Charity is all that we do to reach out to
help those who are victims of a system that is broken. Justice
is all that we do to fix the system.

What are some examples of charity (service) and justice
(advocacy) that you are involved in? That our Church is
doing?

Within your catechetical session, what issue could you
become involved in this year? How could you do it with
your learners?

A Family Connection

Suggest to your learners' families ways that they can make the time and have the courage for both service and advocacy. Many ideas for each are given as we go through the letters of the alphabet ahead.

For everything there is a season,
and a time for everything under heaven.
Loving Lord, help us always to make time for you
and for the gift of our classmates (our family),
time to enjoy,
time to grow,
time to celebrate.
Help us, too, to make time to widen our circle
time to see the people who need our help
time to use our gifts to brighten the lives
of others
time to work with others to make this world
a better place

B

BIBLICAL-BASED

Always begin with Scripture. What is our tradition? What does Scripture say about outreach: service and advocacy? How did Jesus model service ministry?

Use some of these Scripture passages to proclaim and reflect upon during your faith formation sessions in light of our call to serve others:

Exodus 22:21–27   Leviticus 19:9–18
Deuteronomy 24:17–22   Psalm 72
Psalm 9:7–12, 18   Psalm 82
Micah 6:8   Isaiah 58:1–12
Isaiah 61:1–2

Matthew 5:3–12   Matthew 5:38–48
Matthew 6:1–4   Matthew 25:31–46
Mark 2:1–12   Mark 6:34–44
Luke 10:29–37   Luke 15:11–32
John 2:1–11   John 13:1–20
John 15:13   Acts 4:32–35
1 Corinthians 12:22–26   2 Corinthians 8:1–15
James 2:14–17   John 4:19–21

A Family Connection

Suggest to your learners: Each weekend as you talk about the Sunday Scripture readings, have a family discussion about what these readings say about our call to reach out to others and our call to make this world a better place, a more just and peaceful world.

Mary's Magnificat

(which, in addition to a song of great joy, is a call to justice and peace)

My soul magnifies the Lord,
And my spirit rejoices in God my Savior,
For you have looked with favor on the lowliness
  of your servant.
Surely, from now on all generations will call me blessed;
For you, the almighty, have done great things for me,
And holy is your name.
Your mercy is for those who fear you
From generation to generation.
You have shown strength with your arm;
You have scattered the proud in the thoughts of their hearts.
You have brought down the powerful from their thrones,
And lifted up the lowly;
You have filled the hungry with good things,
And sent the rich away empty.
You have helped your servant Israel,
In remembrance of your mercy,
According to the promise you made to our ancestors,
To Abraham and to his descendants forever.

LUKE 1:46–55

C

CONVOY LEARNING

Don't just stay in your classrooms and meeting places to learn. Pile into vans and go to where the needs are. Help your learners meet the people who are in need and be with them. Get to know them personally. Reach out and become friends (if appropriate). For instance,

- Instead of making placemats and holiday decorations and sending them to a senior center, go there. Take your homemade gifts and visit a specific person, gifting them with the gifts and your presence.

- Meet the victims of injustice. Hearing their stories and being with them touches our hearts and spirits and moves us to action. If there is one near your community, visit a Holocaust museum, an African American museum, or traveling exhibits that tell the stories of people who came before us.

A Family Connection
Suggest to your families that they take time to gather the whole family into the car and go to the people, to be with the people you serve.

When you purchase gifts for your parish Giving Tree, be part of the parish representatives who deliver them to the families, the hospitals, etc.

Take food donations to the soup kitchen and help serve the meal. Visit with the people.

Instead of just talking about the gift we have in the diversity of our world (and therefore, our Church), take every opportunity to be a part of the cultural and ethnic heritage of your community, getting to know people and becoming active in various ventures together.

Jesus, Light of the World,
*   help us to bring light to your world.*
Jesus, who befriended the poor,
*   help us to bring light to your world.*
Jesus, who always saw the possible,
*   help us to bring light to your world.*
Jesus, who brought good news,
*   help us to bring light to your world.*

Jesus, who said yes to your Father,
*   help us to bring light to your world.*
Jesus, who sought out those who were hurting,
*   help us to bring light to your world.*
Jesus, Prince of Peace,
*   help us to bring light to your world.*

D

DISCUSS *and* DEBATE

Use every opportunity to discuss the questions and challenges of the day, the signs of the times. Don't shy away from controversial issues. This is the way consciences are formed. When something has happened within your group, neighborhood, in the news, or on television, talk about it. Discuss the issues; try to understand the viewpoint of both sides.

- What happened?
- What were they thinking? Planning?
- Why did people respond as they did?
- What was the outcome?
- What values and priorities stood out?
- Were there other possibilities? Could they have handled things in another way?
- What would you have done?

With older learners, have them explore issues by organizing debates on the two sides of social justice issues.

- Use the technique of an open-ended story as you explore various Catholic belief themes and apply them to everyday living. Invite the learners to discuss the ways they think it should/might end, according to Gospel values.

- Take the Nativity story and write it in modern terms. Discuss some of the injustices that are the same today as they were in the time of Jesus. Then suggest practical ways of overcoming these injustices in today's world.

A Family Connection

Suggest to your families that they make it a common practice to have family conversations/discussions about the questions and challenges of the day, in their home life, their neighborhood, what is happening in the news locally, nationally, internationally. Help parents realize that one of the ways consciences are formed is through conversations with those with faith-filled wisdom and experience. Give parents suggested questions for family reflection and discussion.

Build a family library or visit your local library often for stories that have strong values. Read them together as a family. Discuss how you would feel/act if you were the characters. When events come up in personal, family, or neighborhood life, talk about how the storybook character might have responded in that situation.

Help one another in the family to use the question "How would you feel…?" to evaluate their actions.

Holy and loving God, we come to you for guidance.
Kindle our hearts. Deepen our understanding.
Great and wonderful are your thoughts.
Your ways are true, just, and peace-filled.
Give us your passionate love for all your people.
Make us hearers and doers of your word!

E

EXAMINATION OF CONSCIENCE

When we pray this type of prayer during our catechetical sessions, the reflections and questions can stretch and challenge us beyond our individual lives, our me-and-God relationship. How do we respond to the needs of the poor, those who are neglected, those treated unfairly?

- Are there times when we deliberately leave people out (in our play, our plans, etc.)?

- Do we pick on other people, especially people we don't like, who may be different from us?

- Do we share what we have with those who don't have as much?

- Do we speak up for others when we see things that are wrong?

- Do we show active concern for those in the world who have less than we do?

- Do we ask, "When did we see you hungry?" Are we ready for the response, "As often as you did it for one of my least sisters and brothers, you did it for me"?

- Do we ask, "When did we see you sick?" Are we ready for the response, "As often as you did it for one of my least sisters and brothers, you did it for me"?

A Family Connection

Suggest to your families: This prayer of examination of conscience can conclude family life together each day. Give the families suggested questions to ask themselves, always moving them beyond a God-and-me relationship and toward a spirituality concerned for others, especially the poor and those who are in need.

Loving and all-forgiving God,
  you continually and constantly call us to be reconciled,
  to conversion, to be more aware,
    to leave our safe circles and reach out.
As we are:
Reconciled to another,
  forgive us for the times we have been
    impatient, unkind, and inconsiderate.
Reconciled to all our sisters and brothers,
  forgive us for the times we could have
    cared about those in need and
    instead thought only of ourselves.
Reconciled to you,
  forgive us for the times we failed to put you first.

F

FAMILY-FRIENDLY
service opportunities

There are certainly some types of service/outreach opportunities that your learners will do together. There are some in which only adults will be involved.

There are many that families can do together. There are crucial reasons for doing this; service/outreach is integral to who we are because of our baptism; it is not just for children/youth because they are in faith formation sessions or preparing for the celebration of sacraments. As a catechist, do all you can to encourage and empower your families to be involved in service.

Share with them these guidelines: In planning for family service actions and opportunities:

- Invite, but don't force, all family members to participate.

- Be sure there is a chance, a place, for everyone in the family to have a part, if they choose.

- Make sure the action or project matches the knowledge, skills, interests, needs, and time of everyone in the family.

- Consider actions and projects that connect you with other families or with friends of your children.

- Integrate service with prayer/Scripture and time for reflection together afterward.

- Put "family service" on your family meeting agenda at least once a month, and together decide what to do and how to do it.

- Be sure to affirm one another in all the good that you are doing.

A Family Connection

Share with them these sources for help with ideas for family service opportunities:

Just Give are stories about kids who have made a difference for other kids. Available at justgive.org/be-inspired/inspiring-kids/index.jsp

Volunteering with Your Family (idealist.org/kt/familyvolunteer.html) is a "full-service" Web site with many articles and tips for family service, as well as links for family service ideas.

FamilyCares (www.familycares.org) provides children, families, and religious groups with opportunities to help others in their local and global communities.

Volunteering with Your Family (serviceleader.org/new/volunteers/articles/2003/04/000059.php) gives suggestions about choosing family service projects.

Volunteer Match (volunteermatch.org) helps you locate multitudinous opportunities within your area and according to topic.

Hearts and Minds (heartsandminds.org) is a clearinghouse of helpful information. The mission of this non-profit organization is to combat apathy, offer inspiration, and provide resources for service. They address poverty, the environment, racism, human rights, and other issues. Their goal is to help people get involved in effective, fulfilling ways.

Volunteers of America (voa.org) helps individuals nationwide find volunteer opportunities posted by local nonprofit and public-sector organizations.

Make a Difference Day (usaweekend.com/diffday) includes a database of volunteer opportunities for "Make a Difference Day" each fall.

20 Ways for Teenagers to Help Other People by Volunteering (bygpub.com/books/tg2rw/volunteer.htm) explores many possibilities for service.

Red Cross (redcross.org) has a Web site that contains a section with information on volunteering.

Special Olympics (specialolympics.org) always welcomes volunteers for their projects and activities.

Do Something (dosomething.org) is a national non-profit organization that encourages young people to help build their communities.

The Big Help Toolkit (nick.com/all_nick/specials/big-help/how.jhtml) is a nation-wide program driven by local activities. The focus is on youth, as individuals and in groups, volunteering in their own communities. The Toolkit offers advice on organizing, promoting, and running a project, as well as a list of partnering organizations.

O Most Holy Trinity,
   We see in You the bond of love
   and relationships with which you have
      blessed our class (our family).
   May the love of God the Father surround us
   —so that we can share it.
   May the story of Jesus, God the Son,
      be alive in us (our home),
      so we can live it in our world.
   May the Spirit of Hope, God the Holy Spirit,
      keep us close, sending us forth
      to care for others.
May the blessing of God the Father, the Son,
   and the Holy Spirit,
always guide our decisions and our steps,
   helping us to bring compassion and kindness
      to all we meet,
searching out those who are in need. Amen.

G

GAMES
of simulation

This type of game helps us to imitate the elements of a real-life experience, especially one that is not usually a part of our lives, so that we may experience it, examine it, reflect on it, and, hopefully, apply its lessons to our future behavior.

Some games that might be used within the catechetical setting:

- Have a luncheon with each table having different types (and quantities) of food to simulate the food distribution of the world.

- The Hunger game (this is based on twelve players, but it can be adapted): Players are invited to sit at one of three tables: two at the cookie table (large box of cookies), three at the bread table (one piece of bread), and seven at the cracker table (four crackers). Children will quickly react. Challenge them to work it out. After sufficient time, discuss their experience, helping them to understand that the reality of today's world is that many people have only "crackers" for their meals. Some are more fortunate with "bread." The smallest (and richest) have all the "cookies." Some questions that you might want to discuss are:

» Which group do you think we're in?
» How do you think the world situation got like this?
» Do you think this is fair?
» What could we do?
» What could our leaders do?
» Is there anything we could do to help our leaders?
» What would Jesus say about this?

• For a determined amount of time, pay attention only to a certain segment of the class (those with brown hair, those wearing red, etc.). Ignore everyone else. Then have a discussion regarding everyone's feelings.

A Family Connection

Suggest the following as some things that your learners' families might do:

Use only one pencil (no pens, colored pencils, crayons, magic markers) for three months (some children in some countries have only one for a year).

Plan together your family menu for one week and then shop together for the food you need. Base your meal budget on the current benefits that families receive if they are using U.S. Government food stamps (currently one dollar per meal).

Go to hhs.gov, then search for "poverty guidelines" and select the most recent listing. After you have figured out the current poverty level for your family, together write out a monthly budget using the money suggested by the guidelines. What would it be like to live on this budget? What would have to change?

Loving, remembering God,
  help us to remember.
When we have food,
  help us to remember those who are hungry.
When we are in our warm homes,
  help us to remember the homeless.
When we are healthy and without pain,
  help us to remember those who are sick,
    those who suffer.
When we are loved,
  help us to remember those who are
    forgotten and disrespected.
Loving, remembering God,
  help us to remember enough to act,
    to give
    to reach out
    to do something to make a difference
      for someone who is hurting. Amen.

H

HUNGER CRISIS

Mahatma Gandhi said: "To the millions who have to go without two meals a day, the only acceptable form in which God dare appear is food." Help your young people become more personally aware and act—in small steps—to make a difference in the lives of those who hunger, realizing, too, that there are many forms of hunger in our world today.

- Two Web sites to learn more about the hunger crisis in our world:
    bread.org
    feedingamerica.org

- Sponsor a neighborhood food drive for a local food bank. Do this at a non-holiday time; people are hungry year round.

- Collect pledges in exchange for a one-day fast. (Small children could fast from sweets for a day.)

- Buy trail mix and put it into zipper sandwich bags. Give to a shelter for the homeless so guests have something to eat during the day.

- Organize local food merchants to donate food to shelters. Work with local supermarkets and restaurants to cosponsor a one-day food drive, turning over a percentage of their day's sales to local soup kitchens.

- Suggest/organize your parish to participate in "Souper Bowl Sunday" by asking parishioners to donate one dollar each after football's Super Bowl Sunday. Give the proceeds to a soup kitchen (souperbowl.org).

- As you look at hunger in our world today and the many ways to respond, include the many types of hunger by exploring the Corporal Works of Mercy.

- Collect warm socks for a shelter.

- Collect resources for those in need: food drives, toys for tots, clothing drives, school supplies for low-income children, books/videos for libraries.

- Decorate pillowcases for a homeless shelter.

- Have a baby food drive or baby shower for a women and children's shelter.

- Connect with Habitat for Humanity (habitat.org) to see how you can be a support, advocate, or volunteer.

- Use the Web site Feeding Minds Fighting Hunger (feedingminds.org) to provide the learners with an international interactive experience to begin creating a world free from hunger.

- Kids Can Make a Difference (kidscanmakeadifference. org) is a program for middle and high school youth that focuses on the root causes of hunger and poverty and how youth can help.

A Family Connection

Suggest these ideas to families so they are continuing the work of eliminating hunger with their families:

Have a simple meal once a week and give the money saved to a local soup kitchen, your parish food pantry, or Bread for the World.

Plant gardens with/and for low-income families.

Give up some favorite food each week (ice cream, popcorn, or a trip to your favorite fast food drive-through) and give the savings to a cause that feeds the hungry.

Eat lower on the food chain. Eat less meat; eat more grains and vegetables.

Buy lower on the consumer chain; buy quality items while avoiding costly labels.

Buy fewer items. Look at "what we need" rather than "all we want."

Cook a holiday meal for the homeless.

Learn more about the realities of hunger and material poverty (and some of the efforts to respond to them through Catholic Relief Services [crs.org]). Operation Rice Bowl is a program from CRS that includes prayer, fasting, almsgiving, and learning. If you don't receive all the materials from your parish, go to the above Web site and click on "Get Involved" and "Operation Rice Bowl."

Every year we gaze enviously at the lists of the richest people in the world, wondering what it would be like to have that sort of money. But where would your family be on one of those lists? **Find out at www. globalrichlist.com.** Once you find out, how do you feel? What do you think about some of the suggestions given on this Web site?

Twice a year do a family closet clean-out to collect outgrown clothes and coats. Don't forget toys and gadgets (for both youngsters and moms and dads) that can be shared with homeless shelters or church/community agencies.

Go through your books and donate ones that you're not using any more to a children's hospital.

Decorate pumpkins for Halloween and give to a Head Start center, a shelter for abused women and children, etc.

Build key racks (using small planks of wood and cup hooks) for people moving into homes built by Habitat for Humanity (habitat.org).

In the fall or winter, **plant flower seeds in pots**. In the spring, give the sprouting plants to families moving into homes built by Habitat for Humanity.

O God, who feeds the hungry,
we meet you in food and drink—
 in bread and wine.
We pray that, because of your Bread of Life,
 we may grow more and more to be like you,
  that we may hear the cries of the hungry
  and reach out to all those in need.
Help us, through our caring,
 to offer life and hope to people
  who are hungering for everyday needs,
   for acceptance, for love, for meaning.

I

IMAGINE

Dream of what could be. (Things will only happen if they are first imagined.) Help your learners to use their imagination and dream of the world as God would see it. Dream and visualize a world of peace, a world where life, respect, and human dignity reigns.

Listen to beautiful music and imagine our human family caring for everyone, loving and supporting each other.

- Describe what you see.
- How does this world make you feel?
- What colors appear in this world?
- What sounds do you hear in this world?
- What if we could change our hearts the way we change our minds?
- What if every person gave their best trait to the world?
- What if we carried an idea of hope with us each day?
- What if we had newspapers that only printed Good News?
- What if we were all part of one big country that covered the earth?

A Family Connection

Create an imaginative newspaper, newsletter, bulletin, etc. to share some of the ideas from your learners with your families. Pose the same questions to them. Invite them to dream and imagine as a family!

Holy Spirit, think through me till your ideas are my ideas.

AMY CARMICHAEL (1848-1951)

J

JOURNAL

Invite your learners to keep a journal of their experiences of service and advocacy, linking them to Scripture and Catholic social teaching. Encourage them to compose prayers and reflections of what happens to them as a result of their experiences.

It's always important to take time to reflect on our experiences. What are we learning about ourselves, about those we are serving, about justice/injustice, about the Church's call to service and advocacy? Some questions for reflection:

- What did I feel? What happened in my heart?
- What did I learn about the people I met?
- What did I learn about myself?
- Where/when did I meet Jesus?
- Was I Jesus for someone?
- What did I discover about being a follower of Jesus?
- Will I do anything differently because of this experience?

Let your learners' parents know of their children's journaling experiences. Encourage your youngsters to share some of their thoughts and feelings with their parents and families.

A Family Connection

Invite your families to keep family journals of their family service experiences. Suggest to them some of the same questions you have used with your learners.

Gracious God,
    as I continue through your world,
    gifted in meeting, befriending more and
       more of your family,
I ask and promise, with your help, to do all
    with a compassionate and trusting heart:
       to act justly,
       to love tenderly, and
       to walk closely with you, my God.   Micah 6:8

K

KEEP CONNECTED

Keep connected with the people you serve. Doing *for* is good, but doing *with* is much better. Connecting a real face to our compassionate actions is one concrete way to move us to be committed, not only to charity (service), but also to justice (advocacy).

- Work in a soup kitchen; visit and eat with the people you serve.

- Are there homebound church members who would appreciate a fall or spring clean-up around their home? Share time and refreshments with them.

- Decorate a homeless shelter for Christmas. Stay and visit with the people.

- Visit a nursing home on a regular basis. Visit the same few people so that you establish a relationship with them. Bring them homemade cards and baked goods, or magazines, large-print books, or audio-tape books. Take time to visit with them, play cards, or read to them (if they have limited vision).

A Family Connection

Encourage your families to also "keep connected" as they reach out in service:

Collecting food for your parish food drive is good, but, as a family, be part of the team that delivers it.

Have family members take turns during the week phoning a lonely person to share a friendly "hello" and to listen to the other person for a few minutes.

Volunteer to cook for senior citizens or someone who is grieving.

Deliver Meals on Wheels together as a family.

Is there someone in your parish who needs a ride to church each weekend?

All-caring God,
  allow your care and love to flow through us
and keep us connected
    to those who are hungry and searching,
    to those who feel alone and scared,
    to those who are suffering,
    to those who feel confused
      or are treated unfairly.
Move us to be compassionate and caring
  to all those who are hurting—
    those we meet
    those we haven't yet met.

L

LINK YOUR CELEBRATION
of sacraments and Catholic social teaching

Include the social teaching of the Church in your sacramental preparation programs, especially the Eucharist, the sacrament that calls us continually to unity and service:
The *Catechism of the Catholic Church* reminds us

> The Eucharist commits us to the poor. To receive in truth the Body and Blood of Christ given up for us, we must recognize Christ in the poorest, his brethren: "You have tasted the Blood of the Lord, yet you do not recognize your brother....You dishonor this table when you do not judge worthy of sharing your food someone judged worthy to take part in this meal" (St. John Chrsysostom). (#1397)

This means that we cannot receive Jesus without receiving all members, especially the poor. It has been said that as Catholics we do a very good job of recognizing Jesus on the altar, but at times we fail to recognize Jesus around the altar.

A Family Connection

Invite your families to reflect on these realities and to live them practically in some of these ways:

St. Basil once said that the extra coat and pair of shoes in my closet belongs to the poor. What can you give away?

Bake bread or muffins. After Sunday liturgy, as a family, take them to a homeless shelter. Discuss beforehand what to expect. Stay, eat, and visit with the people.

Begin the custom that when you purchase certain things for your family, you will purchase two—one for your family and one for the poor.

Compose a litany of petitions, similar to the General Intercessions we pray at Mass. Mention the people to whom you are united because you belong to the family of God.

Find out the name of a local family in need of food, clothing, or other supplies. Have each member of the family contribute something to a basket for this family.

As you close the day as a family, invite each member of the family to mention two people (or two groups of people): someone close to them and someone who they do not know but are part of God's family.

Loving God,
through the Church's sacraments,
  we have been anointed
    priest, prophet, and king.

You have made us in your image and likeness,
  called us to co-create with you,
    to image you in this world.

Let our reflection of you
  be loving and forgiving,
  tender and kind,
  ever present to those in need,
  ever compassionate,
  always peaceful. Amen.

M

MEMORIAL CELEBRATIONS

Using your local library and the internet, do some research. Make a calendar and then take time to remember and prayerfully celebrate the lives of those who have gone before us who have been prophets and witnesses to the social teachings of our Church, for example, Archbishop Oscar Romero, the North American women martyred in El Salvador (December 2), Sr. Dorothy Stang, Dorothy Day, and Rosa Parks.

On your calendar, too, place:

- National and Church celebrations of justice or service, such as:
  - » National Migration Week (beginning of January)
  - » Martin Luther King Jr. Day
    (Third Monday of January)
  - » Operation Rice Bowl (during the lenten season)
  - » World Health Day (April 17)
  - » Earth Day (April 22)
  - » the day the Supreme Court declared racial segregation in schools unconstitutional (May 17)

» No Nukes Day (August 6)
» Civil Rights Day (August 12)
» Women's Equality Day (August 26)
» International Peace Day (September 21)
» World Food Day (October 16)
» UN International Day for the Eradication of Poverty (October 17)
» United Nations Day (October 24)
» Human Rights Day (December 10)
» the day the Bill of Rights was ratified (December 15)
» National and Global Youth Service Day (ysa.org/nysd)

- Dates of importance to people of various ethnic groups, for instance:
  » Feast of St. Patrick (March 17)
  » Feast of St. Joseph (March 19)
  » Asian/Pacific American Heritage Week (First Week of May)
  » Holocaust Remembrance Day (ushmm.org/remembrance/dor)
  » African Freedom Day (May 25)
  » Mexican Independence Day (September 16)
  » American Indian Day (fourth Friday of September)
  » Our Lady of Guadalupe (December 12)

- Church feast days reflecting the cultural diversity of our Church or raising justice issues:
  » Kateri Tekakwitha (July 14)
  » Maximillian Kolbe (August 14)
  » St. Francis of Assisi (October 4)
  » Our Lady of Guadalupe (December 12)

A Family Connection

Have your learners make these calendars to take home and place in prominent places where their families will always see them. Send home family ideas for prayer, rituals, and celebrations for these days of remembrance.

For the people of God who challenge us,
*   we thank you, loving God.*
For the people of God who encourage us,
*   we thank you, loving God.*
For the people of God who comfort us,
*   we thank you, loving God.*
For the people of God who inspire us,
*   we thank you, loving God.*
For the people of God who wake us up,
*   we thank you, loving God.*
For the people of God who quiet us,
*   we thank you, loving God.*
For the people of God who motivate us,
*   we thank you, loving God.*
For the people of God who call us to more,
*   we thank you, loving God.*
For the people of God who are disciples of Jesus,
*   we thank you, loving God.*
For the people of God who call us to be
*   disciples of Jesus,*
*   we thank you, loving God.*

N

NOTICE THE NEWS
and television

Use your local newspapers and television programs to help children/youth grow up thinking globally and acting locally. Place a world map or globe in a prominent place in your catechetical setting and refer to it often.

Help your learners analyze the real-life situations of Catholic social teaching found in local and world news and in their favorite television programs. In which activities and events do we see evidence of the principles of the Church's social teachings? Where are the principles of justice, equality, and respect ignored?

Frequently use the newspaper headlines to compose a litany of General Intercessions during your prayer services.

A Family Connection
Send home ideas for your learners' families:

Grow in your awareness of our connectedness. Use world map placemats for family dinners.

Use the newspaper headlines to compose a litany of General Intercessions before your family dinner.

Create a Good News bulletin board in your kitchen. Cut out newspaper articles or print articles from online about people living the Church's social teachings around the world.

God of the Nations, you are Creator of all.
  You created us as one,
  sisters and brothers of all,
    connected to each other.
If one is rejoicing, it is our happiness,
If one is hurting, it is our sorrow
  and   we are called to help.
Make us your followers, ready to always care
  and work so that your kingdom
may come on this earth as in heaven. Amen.

OBSERVE
EARTH DAY

Catholic social teaching calls us to care for God's creation. Earth Day is celebrated once a year and reminds us that there are many practical observances and actions that individuals, groups, and families can do every day so that we become a simpler, more careful society.

- Recycle whenever possible.
- Volunteer to start or help with a community garden.
- Volunteer to maintain local parks and wilderness.
- Observe the birthday of the ice cream cone (September 22). This invention made it possible to not waste the container.
- Read books like the *Little House* series (by Laura Ingalls Wilder) to learn how people used to live creatively with much less. How can we live more simply today?
- Log on to the UNAWE Web site (unawe.org). UNAWE is an international outreach program that uses the beauty and scale of the universe to inspire very young children in underprivileged environments. The goals

of the program are not specifically religious, but awakening the minds of children to the wonders of the universe goes hand in hand with opening their minds and hearts to the God who is the creator of all of these wonders. The Web site offers resources and plans that can easily be adapted to a catechetical setting.

- Participate in your community's annual "City Clean-Up Day." If your city doesn't have one, contact your city council and ask them to plan one.

- Visit The Sierra Club (sierraclub.org), especially the "Local" tab, which helps people stay in touch with events and issues in their own area.

- Log on to the following Web sites for information and suggestions for action to care for God's creation:
Carbon Footprint (carbonfootprint.com)
Friends of the Earth (foe.org)
Global Stewards (globalstewards.org)
The Green Guide (thegreenguide.com)
Hooked on Nature (hookedonnature.org)
Worldwatch Institute (worldwatch.org)

A Family Connection
Help children to take ideas home to their families to celebrate the Earth all year long:

Mend and repair, rather than discard and replace.

Pick up litter along highways and near your home.

Instead of buying more, **use your local library**.

Shop at local stores and thrift stores, buy from local producers, eat at neighborhood restaurants.

Challenge children to reduce the electric bill.

Learn through the internet about worldwide water usage and shortage (waterfootprint.org). Estimate your usage. How can your family use less?

For each new item you buy, give away a similar item to someone in need.

Check some of the Web sites that encourage a simplicity of lifestyle:
Affluenza (affluenza.org)
Alternatives for Simple Living (simpleliving.org)
50 Possible Ways to Challenge Over-Commercialism (earthhealing.info/fifty.htm)
New American Dream (newdream.org)
The Simple Living Network (simpleliving.net/main)

Creator God,
the psalmist reminds us that
"the heavens are telling the glory of God,
and the earth proclaims God's handiwork."

How awesome is your gift of life to us,
the mystery of our holiness
and who we are called to be,
as your creatures in the web of life.

Call us, challenge us more and more
to be aware of our connections—
of the sacredness of earth
and all your creation.
Thank you for these gifts;
we pledge our responsible care. Amen.

P

PLACE PEACE
AT THE TOP *of your*
list of priorities

You, of course, have much to do each time you gather with your learners. It's easy to say that peace is a priority, but there is a way of infusing a value, a virtue throughout all your endeavors, of having that deep reality saturate everything. Peace should always be a guiding value in all that happens in your catechetical setting and in all your discussions of how a Catholic lives and is called to change the world.

Consider these actions with your learners:

- Invite learners to keep an Inventory of Peace. When and where do they most feel the lack of peace? When do they feel "in conflict"? Why? How could these conflicts be resolved peacefully?

- Spread peace in any way you can: A smile can light up another person's day (and your own).

- Always look for ways to cooperate rather than compete.

- When anyone does something—no matter how small—to increase peace in any aspect of life, applaud them. Let them know how grateful you are for their courage and example.

- When you see a success story for peace, spread the word about it. Write it up for your local newspaper; tell your friends; call it in to a radio talk show.

- Make creative posters about peace. Ask your neighborhood businesses and stores if they would put one in their window.

- Read the story of *Sadako and the Thousand Paper Cranes* (Eleanor Coerr, Puffin Modern Classics, 2004). Make paper peace cranes. Send them with letters to the President of the United States and other world leaders asking that they work for world peace. Decorate your stationery with the words that are on the base of Sadako's statue, "This is our cry, this is our prayer: Peace in the world."

- Celebrate the International Day of Peace (September 21). In 1981, the United Nations passed a resolution declaring this day as an opportunity for individuals, organizations, and nations to create acts of peace on a shared date, hopefully moving toward more of an awareness of cultivating peace all the time.

- Organize a Friday vigil for peace for one hour in your parish.

- For resources on prayer for peace—as well as up-to-date news items—check the Pax Christi USA Web site (paxchristiusa.org).

- United for Peace and Justice (unitedforpeace.org) is a collaboration of national and international peace and social justice organizations and scores of local places of worship, peace centers, and community organizations. A look at the site will give tangible evidence of the many Americans who are committed to and actively working for peace in our world.

- The Rumors of Peace Newsletter of the Nonviolent Peaceforce can be found at nonviolentpeaceforce.org. The following story comes from the site.

A Native American grandfather was talking to his grandson about the tragedy of 9/11. He said, "I feel as if I have two wolves fighting in my heart. One wolf is vengeful, angry, and violent. The other one is loving and compassionate."

The grandson asked, "Which wolf will win the fight in your heart?"

The grandfather answered, "The one I feed."

- Amber and Ryan Amundson, the wife and brother of Craig Amundson, who was killed at the Pentagon on 9/11, fulfilled their pledge to help create an organization of family members of 9/11 victims who seek peaceful and just responses, not war, to the criminal attacks: Peaceful Tomorrows (peacefultomorrows.org).

- Our prayers for peace can be translated into action in numerous ways. One concrete way is keeping in touch with our Congressional representatives. E-mail addresses for the House of Representatives can be found at: house.gov. The e-mail addresses for our Senators are at senate.gov.

- Plant a Peace Pole or have a World Peace Flag Ceremony (worldpeace.org).

- Do your part to contribute to a culture of peace wherever

you are. Find numerous ideas for a global movement for a culture of peace (WeWantPeaceOnEarth.com).

- A Web site filled with peace resources is bigpicture-smallworld.com/movies/winningpeace.html. Beginning here will start you at a short but powerful video reflection on war and peace. You will then move to a Web site with numerous links to some of the many organizations who have committed themselves to make a difference in changing the world. There is a guide for teachers designed to expand, deepen, and enrich a movie produced by BigPictureSmallWorld, Inc. Some of the suggested discussion questions are:

  » What causes peace?

  » Where does peace begin?

  » There is an ancient Chinese proverb, "Unless we change our direction, we are likely to end up where we are headed." Where is the world headed?

  » If a country gets what it prepares for, what happens when that country prepares for war? If a country were to prepare for peace what would it get? How does a country prepare for peace? How do you prepare for peace?

- Since peace-making isn't a one-day event, betterworld-calendar.com is a helpful site of days to celebrate hope for a better world. This Web site features holidays and commemorations for almost every day of the year. Some of the days you will find are:

  January 1: Global Family Day
  February 21: Language Day
  March 21: End Racism Day
  May 1: Workers Day
  May 21: Dialogue Day
  June 20: Refugee Day

June 26: End Torture Day
July 12: Simplicity Day
September 12: Interdependence Day

A Family Connection

Encourage your families to live peace each day. Many of the above ideas and resources would also be applicable to them. In addition, share these suggestions with them:

Talk together as a family: What stands in the way of strengthening relationships in your family? For what do you need to ask forgiveness from another family member?

Talk about the many ingredients needed for a successful recipe. What are the needed ingredients for a recipe for family peace? What are the needed ingredients for a recipe for world peace?

Have regular family meetings to make family decisions, to talk about any conflicts. A shared approach to making decisions, plans, and resolving conflicts is probably the single most important mechanism for promoting peace and cooperation in the home.

Make a family decision that no "war or violent toys" will have a place in your home.

As a family, **create a peace toy or game**.

Have a family discussion about the type of language, the tone of speech that happens in your home. Is it peaceful? Are there things you might do to make it more peaceful?

Volunteer for a service project for peace in your community (serviceforpeace.org).

Three prayer resources from the United States Catholic Conference of Bishops are, A Rosary for Peace, A Scriptural Rosary for Justice and Peace, and A Prayer for Peace. These are available at 1-800-235-8722 or usccbpublishing.org.

Prayer for Peace
(attributed to St. Francis of Assisi)

Lord, make me an instrument of your peace.
Where there is hatred, let me sow your love,
Where there is injury, pardon,
Where there is doubt, faith,
Where there is despair, hope,
Where there is darkness, light,
Where there is sadness, joy.
O Divine Master, grant that I may not so much seek to be consoled as to console,
to be understood as to understand,
to be loved, as to love;
for it is in giving that we receive,
it is in pardoning that we are pardoned,
it is in dying that we are born to eternal life.

Q

QUIET TIME
for reflection

The following quotes (and many others) can be used individually by your youngsters and youth in their journals and for sharing during your prayer time:

> "The opposite of love is not hatred; it is indifference." (Daniel Berrigan, SJ)

> "In the evening of this life you will be judged according to your love." (St. John of the Cross)

> "When I give food to the poor, they call me a saint. When I ask why the poor have no food they call me a communist." (Dom Helder Camara)

> Think globally, act locally.

> "We have all known the long loneliness and we have learned that the only solution is love and that love comes with community." (Dorothy Day)

How can I love God whom I cannot see, if I don't love my brother or sister whom I can see? (1 John 4:20)

"If you are preoccupied with people who are talking about the poor, you scarcely have time to talk to the poor." (Mother Teresa)

A Family Connection

Include these quotes (and others) in your notes and newsletters to your parents, suggesting that they be used at home for quiet reflection or family sharing.

In his book *Praying by Hand* (HarperSanFrancisco, 1991), Fr. Basil Pennington suggests five new decades of the rosary to reflect contemporary social justice concerns: Jesus Feeds the Hungry; Jesus Heals the Sick; Jesus Respects Women; Jesus Reaches Out and Touches Outcasts; and Jesus Honors the Despised. Use these mysteries to meditate and pray the rosary.

R

RESEARCH

Within your catechetical setting, look into companies and manufacturers from whom your learners' families make their purchases, companies from which your parish makes purchases. Are they in compliance with just wages, safe conditions, and fair labor laws? Do they utilize sweatshops? Frequently you will hear about unjust practices in the newspaper or in television reports. You can also go to responsibleshopper.org, a Web site that maintains a directory of many major companies and their business practices.

After your research, do all you can as a group, given age-appropriateness (talk to local owners, letter writing to CEOs of corporations, letters to the editors of local newspapers, boycotting, etc.), to request that they conform to fair labor practices.

(There are many issues that will surface when you look at the world through the eyes of Gospel values. What do you want to advocate for? Research and then let your voice be heard.)

At the same time, research organizations who are working for justice and peace, who are supporting the social teachings of the Church.

- The Campaign for Human Development, sponsored by the U.S. bishops, funds employment and community development projects for the poor. How can you support or work with them?

- Heifer International (heifer.org) is a long-standing organization working for ending hunger and caring for the earth.

- Bread for the World (bread.org) is a nationwide Christian citizens movement seeking justice for the world's hungry people by lobbying our nation's decision makers.

- Children's Defense Fund (childrensdefense.org) is a child advocacy group.

- Catholic Relief Services (crs.org) is the official international humanitarian agency of the U.S. Catholic community. Their goal is to alleviate suffering and provide assistance to people in need in more than 100 countries, without regard to race, religion, or nationality.

- Catholic Charities USA (catholiccharitiesusa.org) works throughout the nation helping individuals, families, and communities, working at the root causes of poverty and dysfunction.

- Pax Christi (paxchristi.net or paxchristiusa.org) is a Catholic peace movement working on a global scale on a wide variety of issues in the fields of human rights, human security, disarmament and demilitarisation, a just world order, and religion and violent conflict.

Support the work of groups, both domestic and international, that monitor national and international responses to injustice (poverty, hunger, health care, etc.), such as:
Food First (foodfirst.org)
Oxfam International (oxfam.org)

A Family Connection
Let your families know about this research project. Invite them to join you in the research. Keep them up-to-date on your research. Invite them to join you in:

- contacting companies
- advocating for justice in working conditions
- becoming acquainted with the many organizations working for justice and peace

Jesus, who was a carpenter,
  bless the workers.
Jesus, who was homeless,
  bless the wanderers.
Jesus, who blessed the loaves and fishes,
  bless the hungry.
Jesus, who was accused unjustly,
  bless those who are treated unfairly.
Jesus, who suffered,
  bless those who are in pain.
Jesus, who was crucified,
  bless those who are afraid.
Jesus, who was raised to new life on Easter day,
  move us to action to be your prophets
    in today's world.

S

SKILLS BUILDING

Help your learners to learn and to deepen the skills that are needed for service/outreach and advocacy:

- listening skills (e.g., listening when visiting the elderly).
- skills for conversing as you meet new people. For example:
  - » skills in working with those with special needs.
  - » skills in being with people with whom they usually do not relate. Young people who have had no preparation prior to volunteering in a homeless shelter or soup kitchen and come away thinking, "Gee, street people are as dirty and smelly as they look on TV" haven't learned the real and correct message from the experience. They need adequate preparation beforehand.
- skills of letter-writing, especially to newspapers and members of state and national legislatures. (The seventh graders of St. Genevieve School in Thibodaux, Louisiana, wrote a booklet giving helpful guidelines, "Write Makes Might." To contact them: 985-447-9291.)

- the virtue of empathy and the gift of joy. Coming up against injustice, hungers, and needs can be sad. While we certainly want to listen and not make light of the situation (and work for advocacy for change), we also want to bring God's joy to those we meet. The motto of the Little Brothers of the Poor is "bread and flowers." Their motivation is to always recognize the whole person when they visit the elderly poor. They realize that the "necessities" of life are more than basic food and shelter. It also includes nourishment for the human spirit; that includes joy.

A Family Connection

Many of these skills, of course, are learned in everyday life, in family life. Share with your parents how these skills—skills that can be used in many situations—are so crucial to who we are as disciples of Jesus. Give your families continual examples of how the learners are practicing the skills in your catechetical setting. Suggest ideas of things they can do as a family (things they are already doing) that deepen these skills.

Creative God,
You have given us the power and the ability
  to make another smile,
  to help those in need
    —large and small,
  to be a healing presence for those
    who are hurting,
  to bring justice where there is oppression,
  to bring comfort where there is difficulty,
  to sow seeds of peace wherever we go
    and always, always,
  to be kind, to show compassion, and to love.
Be with us as we deepen our skills
  to grow more and more into your disciples
    so that people will know you
      —through us—
and this world will be a reflection
  of your kingdom.

T

TELL THE STORIES

Weave into your catechetical sessions time to frequently read, research, reflect on, and learn about the stories of service and outreach in our tradition.

- Search the Scriptures for stories of the prophets, Jesus, and the early Christians.

- Young people today know all the movie, TV, and sports stars. Help them to learn about and be very familiar with people from our tradition and human history: St. John Chrysostom, St. Vincent de Paul, St. Frances Cabrini, St. Elizabeth Anne Seton, Mother Teresa, Martin Luther King, Ghandi, Dr. Tom Dooley, Dorothy Day, and others.

- Who are your family members and relatives, church/ parish and community members, people in the news who have lived a life of service and justice? Invite people from your parish or your local community who model servant leadership and ministry to speak to your group.

A Family Connection

Invite your families to tell the stories. Television has become the story-teller for today's generation. Help your families to regain their proper place as the story-teller for the stories that matter.

Suggest Scripture stories for family sharing.

Provide Internet resources or biographies of people who have been examples of service and outreach to others.

Encourage families to watch the news for good news: stories of people who are living lives of service, who take, even a moment, to reach out, to share their lives with others.

Invite them to tell the stories (at dinnertime or bedtime) of family members, relatives, and neighbors who have been examples of service.

As families tell these stories, invite them to **create a list of family heroes/mentors.** Invite them to place the list on the refrigerator, near the family Bible, or in a prominent place in their home, and to add to it as the story-telling continues.

We give thanks, most loving God,
for the saints and prophets who went before us
   who have been witnesses
   who have touched our hearts
   and lived the story,
we praise you, our ever-living God.

We give thanks, most loving God,
for the saints and prophets who live among us
   whose lives and gifts and failings are
      intertwined with ours,
      who teach us the story
         by their faithfulness,
we praise you, our ever-living God.

We give thanks, most loving God,
for the saints and prophets who live beyond us
   who challenge us
   whose lives magnanimously live the Story,
   who beckon us to transform the
      world with them,
we praise you, our ever-living God.

U

UTILIZE HELPFUL
RESOURCES

There are many resources available today that provide numerous ideas for connecting children/youth with Catholic social teaching and the living out of our Gospel values. Just a few:

Go and Do Likewise: Catholic Social Teaching in Action by Mia Crosthwaite (Twenty-Third Publications, 2006)

Stick Your Neck Out: A Street-Smart Guide to Creating Change in Your Community and Beyond by John Graham (Berret-Koehler Publishers, Inc., 2005)

How to Make the World a Better Place: 116 Ways You Can Make a Difference by Jeffrey Hollender, with Linda Catling (Norton, 1995)

The Kid's Guide to Service Projects by Barbara Lewis (Free Spirit Publishing, 1995)

Activities for Catholic Social Teaching: A Resource Guide for Teachers and Youth Ministers by James McGinnis (Ave Maria Press, 2006)

Learning to Serve, Serving to Learn by Joseph Moore (Ave Maria Press, 1994)

Sharing Catholic Social Teaching: Challenges and Directions
(USCCB Publishing Services, available in Spanish)

*Who are My Sisters and Brothers? A Catholic Educational
Guide for Understanding and Welcoming Immigrants and
Refugees* (USCCB Publishing Services)

Cyberschoolbus (un.org/cyberschoolbus)

Education for Justice (educationforjustice.org)

Free the Children (freethechildren.org)

Global Dimension…the world in your classroom
(www.globaldimension.org.uk)

The Institute for Peace and Justice (ipj-ppj.org)

Jigsaw Classroom (jigsaw.org)

Multicultural Pavilion (edchange.org/multicultural)

National Association for Multicultural Education
(nameorg.org)

Resources for Catholic Educators
(silk.net/RelEd/justice.htm)

Office for Social Justice, Archdiocese of Saint Paul and
Minneapolis (osjspm.org)—has a special section for
religious educators

Social Justice Resources for Educators, Catholic Diocese
of Joliet, Illinois (paxjoliet.org/justeach)

Teaching and Learning for Peace
(tlpeace.org.au/index.htm)

Teaching Tolerance (tolerance.org)

A Family Connection

Suggest these resources for your families:

365 Ways to Change the World by Michael Norton (Free
Press, 2007)

Teaching Kids to Care and Share by Jolene Roehlkepartain (Abingdon Press, 2000)

Teaching Your Kids to Care: How to Discover and Develop the Spirit of Charity in Your Children by Deborah Spaide (Replica Books, 2002)

Raising Kids Who Will Make a Difference: Helping Your Family Live with Integrity, Value Simplicity, and Care for Others by Susan G. Vogt (Loyola Press, 2002)

Donate Your Birthday (donateyourbirthday.org/index.php/home)

Be, Live, Buy Different (ibuydifferent.org)

Kids Who Care (geocities.com/kidswhocare)

The Lion and Lamb Peace Arts Center, Bluffton University (bluffton.edu/lionlamb)

New Songs for Peace (newsongsforpeace.org)

The Peace Company (thepeacecompany.com)

The World Peace Prayer Society (worldpeace.org)

God of Wisdom,
  you surround us with the astounding and
    magnificent wisdom you have given to
      your people.
Gives us the eyes of Jesus
  that we may see others beyond the new ideas.
Give us the ears of Jesus
  that we may hear all the needs
    that remain unspoken.
Give us the voice of Jesus
  that we may speak to our world your dream,
    your vision for the kingdom.

V

VOICE YOUR OPINIONS

Having studied the principles of Catholic social teaching, communicate, communicate, communicate: phone calls, letters, e-mails to TV stations, newspapers, your legislators. Even small children can understand and write about many of the issues, such as peace and respect for creation.

Check with the Web site of your state's Catholic Conference legislative network. They usually list all the contact information for national and local legislators. (To find your state's Catholic Conference, go to nasccd.org.)

- Become familiar with pending legislation or proposals that affect people's basic needs and address justice issues. Keep in touch with these organizations for information about important legislation affecting basic needs:

  Network: A National Catholic Social Justice Lobby
    (networklobby.org)
  Children's Defense Fund
    (childrensdefense.org)

- Write to your legislators concerning an issue that is important to Catholic social teaching, such as asking them to sponsor a bill to abolish the death penalty.

- Write letters to advocate for programs addressing hunger issues through Bread for the World (bread.org).

- Write letters to advocate for human rights through Amnesty International (amnesty.org or amnestyusa.org). Amnesty International works for human rights, especially in campaigns to end the death penalty, to abolish torture, to stop violence against women, to protect the right to food, and to stop weapons proliferation.

- Write letters to television executives (and sponsors of television programs) asking that they seriously look at the violence that is promoted on television programming today.

- Write letters to the advertising division of a magazine or a corporation if you have found that their commercials and ads stereotype some people in our world today; if their ads are misleading; if their ads are not respectful.

- Encourage your parish to use its purchasing power to support businesses who demonstrate concern for values and social concerns and let them know why you are supporting them. Boycott companies whose business practices are unjust or discriminatory, are detrimental to the environment, or who take advantage of the poor. Let these companies know why you are boycotting them.

A Family Connection

Encourage your families to let their voices be heard, individually and as a family. Remind them of the reality that when a company, a manufacturer, or a store has been involved in unfair practices toward its employees or has engaged in practices that are harmful to the care of our earth, and those practices were brought to light, boycotts have been found to be an effective form of our power as customers, as consumers.

Encourage families to make a plan—as a family—to boycott the store or the product(s), and then write letters, letting the companies and stores know the reasons for their boycott.

At the same time, use your family purchasing power to support organizations and businesses who demonstrate social concern in your community, the country, and our world—and let them know why you are supporting them.

Come, Holy Spirit,
  Open our ears to listen,
  Open our mouths to speak,
  Open our hands to work for justice and
    peace in your world.
Continually change us.
Help us spread your Word, your peace.
Work in us to transform the world,
  for the dignity and respect for all.

W

WIDEN YOUR WORLD

Our world is getting smaller every day. Are we aware of everyone, of how connected we are?

From magazines or calendars, display pictures of people from other cultures in your catechetical meeting place. Help your learners identify with others who live in different places and circumstances, but who are much like themselves.

- Collect meal prayers from many cultures, many countries. Put them together into a booklet to be taken home and kept and used at their family meals.

- Connect to the missionary network. We learn much about the Third World from travelers and especially missionaries, who usually publish magazines (e.g., *Maryknoll*).

- Point out stereotypes and cultural misinformation depicted in some of today's movies, TV shows, computer games, and other media. Help children/youth recognize biases and examine them, and help them look for the accurate information.

- Be honest about differences. Do not tell children/
youth that we are all the same; we're not. We're one
and equal, but not all the same. We're diverse; that's
the beauty of God's creation. We experience the world
in different ways, and those experiences matter. Help
children/youth understand the viewpoints of others.

A Family Connection

Give suggestions to your families of fun and significant ways
to widen their world.

Trace your family tree. For many of us, that may only
get us to Europe, but it's a start.

Learn a language together as a family. It's one of the
best ways to learn something of the soul of a people.

Many organizations have global ties and the organizations are numerous! **Choose an organization** that
interests your family.

There are magnificent and meaningful children's books
today that open our world to the realities of other cultures, other worlds. **Read together** as a family.

As a family, where age-appropriate, **read the newspaper** or weekly news magazines such as *Time* or
Newsweek and look for justice issues in our country
and world.

Look for TV news shows and documentaries that focus
on justice issues. As a family, talk about what you saw
and heard. What is happening? How does it affect us?
What can we do?

Look at the cultural diversity reflected in your
home's artwork, music, and literature. Add something

new. Give multicultural dolls, toys, or games as gifts. Bookmark diversity Web sites on your computer.

Often we consider ourselves "the norm"; anyone who isn't like us is different, is "the other." **Try to view people** you see or meet who might be different from you (in educational background, richer, poorer, who use a different language, are a different race, etc.) not as "the other," but just as they are, as people in the human family. What have you learned about them? from them?

Reflect on—and perhaps do something about—how your children (and you) define "normal." Expand the definition. Visit playgrounds where a variety of children are present, people of different races, ethnicities, socioeconomic backgrounds, etc.

When someone says or does something that reflects biases or embraces stereotypes, don't let the moment pass. Help everyone in the family examine if the joke or statement is funny, is accurate. Help them to put themselves in the person's shoes. How would they feel?

Faithful Creator, you have made us a
part of a splendid—and connected—world.

Move us to action
so we may always see the faces of our
worldwide sisters and brothers.

Move us to action
so that we do not care for just ourselves

but for all those in need,
even those we do not know.

Move us to action
so that we don't exclude
anyone different from us
but see everyone as sisters and brothers,
all one family.

Move us to action
so that we speak for those who
cannot speak for themselves,
the poor,
those treated unfairly,
and who suffer injustice.

Move us to action
so there will someday be justice and peace
for all.

X

XPLORE WHY WE ENGAGE IN SERVICE
and advocacy

Always connect the caring, service, outreach, and advocacy actions and projects of your catechetical program (and your parish) with the biblical call, the Church's strong tradition of Catholic social teaching, and our baptismal promises to be a people for others. We're not just doing it because we have extra time, because it's a nice thing to do; it's who we are as disciples of Jesus.

A Family Connection

Don't just give families suggestions of what to do. Connect. Link. Give a short supporting scriptural passage with each suggestion. Cite a brief Catholic social teaching from our long tradition that relates to the action. Continually recall that our baptism is ongoing in all we do; it is not a one-time sacrament.

We believe in God
  who created us to be one,
  who surprises us with gifts
    we could never imagine,
  gifts, not for ourselves,
    but to be used for others.

We believe in Jesus,
    friend of the poor and
    searcher of those in need,
  who beckons us to follow him
    and do as he did.

We believe in the Holy Spirit
  who watches over us in compassionate caring,
  who calls us by name,
    sending us forth to bring peace,
      compassion, and reconciliation to all.

We believe in the church,
  a sacrament of Jesus in today's world,
    working for justice,
    living in hope,
    preaching and living the Good News
  of God's unconditional, amazing love.

Y

YOUR WITNESS

Do your learners, first and foremost, know that the call of the Gospel to serve... "to feed the hungry, to clothe the naked, to shelter the homeless, to welcome the stranger..." (Matthew 25:45) is integral to our lives because they see it in you?

They constantly see you as a follower of Jesus because of the way you relate to them, because of your respect for each individual. They witness you as a disciple who knows and lives the Gospel, the Catholic social teachings of our Church, because of your kindness toward others, your involvement in making our world a better place.

A Family Connection

Constantly affirm your parents. (Often they only hear from teachers and catechists when there is a problem. Often they only hear of things they could be doing better.) Affirm them in what a wonderful job they are doing as Catholic parents. Remind them that their children are growing to be committed disciples, willing to be people of compassion, willing to change the world because of the lives of self-sacrifice they see lived by their parents. They experience the love of Jesus in how they are cared for unconditionally by their parents.

Spirit of God,
Encircle us with the fire of Christ's love,
Help us to listen to God's word alive
    in and around us,
Breathe into our hearts new life,
    new courage,
    new hope.
Send us forth to proclaim the Good News
    by how we live,
Call us to open ourselves to the needs of others,
Work through us to change the face of the earth.
    Amen.

Z

ZOOM IN *on parish and community opportunities*

Don't just plan service and outreach opportunities for children and youth. (That might tell them that service and advocacy is something that they do only because they're young learners.)

Connect the children and young people with the opportunities that are already going on in your parish and community so that they are working side-by-side with many committed adult Christians who model that this is a forever way of life.

A Family Connection

As you give suggestions to families, suggest that they don't always just plan service and outreach opportunities for their family working alone. Some suggestions will, of course, lend themselves to that venue; those will be good experiences for them.

At the same time, there will be many suggestions where

families can connect with another family, or two or three. They can connect with the opportunities that are already going on in the parish and community so that families are serving with many Christians in community.

Thank you, Gracious God,
Most Holy Trinity, that you have made us
    a community.
We are blessed that we don't do this alone.
We are called to work in your name,
    to build the reign of God,
        together…with your family.

We pray that we may continue, Gracious God,
    to walk in the footsteps of Jesus—together.
Together we can do much more
    than we could do alone.
In your Wisdom, that is how you created us
    as a community.
Thank you, Gracious God.

FROM JESUS...TO US

As a young family left church one Sunday morning, their seven-year-old daughter asked, "How come Jesus fed the 5,000 when they were hungry and now he lets millions of people go hungry?"

Before her mom and dad could answer, their twelve-year-old son responded, "God was in his prime in those days. There were all kinds of miracles when Jesus was alive."

Perhaps the seven-year-old's question is the question of many today—in the face of the suffering that happens in much of our world.

The answer is in our hands. It is close to us, it is easy to see in our Gospel call and the social teachings of our church. The answer is in our hands. In the words of St. Therese of Avila: "Christ has no hands, but yours."